HERE'S WHAT PEOPLE ARE SAYING ABOUT
TARTESSOS AND OTHER CITIES

"In *Tartessos*, Claire Millikin takes us deep into both the imagined and real cities and houses of the mind. Memory strikes an urgent chord in her work, haunted by the family and strangers who step in and out of a world that is lost and found and lost again. "I was born and raised in that country of damage/ behind the rains," Millikin tells us, as she
considers the tension between the elegiac and the erotic. Tartessos is a stunning mix of evocative beauty and remarkably fine-tuned language."

— Kathleen Ellis
author of *Vanishing Act* (2007)

"Tartessos was a semi-mythical harbor city on the south coast of the Iberian Peninsula. The Tartessians were important tradespeople, most notably of gold, silver, tin and bronze. In Claire Millikin's *Tartessos and Other Cities,* she offers poetry that is metal-rich, that solders narratives and images of precious value. With a deft hand, final couplets in poems like "Tift County, Georgia" become lasting epigrams: "Only the surface layer / of history passes for truth." These poems seek out uneasy passages into tombs where the speaker examines unsettling memories of human activity in the past that are enacted anew before the reader's eyes. Using passive and active remote sensing abilities, Millikin's poems are amulets of hope, endurance and survival."

— Sean Frederick Forbes
author of *Providencia: A Book of Poems* (2013)

"The project of Claire Millikin's *Tartessos and Other Cities* is to come to terms with the condition of being cut off from origins— the timeless subject of exile. These poems enact the difficult work of retracing one's way through imagination to lost home and lost memory, landscape calling out to be mended. The book's honesty and precision in looking back achieves remarkable transformation— the possibility of seeing the present moment anew."

— Debra Nystrom
author of *Night Sky Frequencies New and Selected Poems* (2016)

T0083739

tARtessos
AND OTHER CitieS

TARTESSOS
AND OTHER CITIES

Poems by Claire Millikin

Introduction by
Fred Marchant

NEW YORK
www.2leafpress.org

P.O. Box 4378
Grand Central Station
New York, New York 10163-4378
editor@2leafpress.org
www.2leafpress.org

2LEAF PRESS
is an imprint of the
Intercultural Alliance of Artists & Scholars, Inc. (IAAS),
a NY-based nonprofit 501(c)(3) organization that promotes
multicultural literature and literacy.
www.theiaas.org

Copyright © 2016 by Claire Millikin Raymond

Author Photo: Elisabeth Hogeman
Book design and layout: Gabrielle David

Library of Congress Control Number: 2015941267
ISBN-13: 978-1-940939-42-1 (Paperback)
ISBN-13: 978-1-940939-43-8 (eBook)

10   9   8   7   6   5   4   3   2   1

Published in the United States of America

First Edition | First Printing

2LEAF PRESS trade distribution is handled by University of Chicago Press / Chicago Distribution Center (www.press.uchicago.edu) 773.702.7010. Titles are also available for corporate, premium, and special sales. Please direct inquiries to the UCP Sales Department, 773.702.7248.

To the memory of Henry Braun, and
for the D'Silva family

Tartessos was once a city on the Guadalquivir, in Andalusia, Spain. But the city vanished, and was thought to be a myth until archeological excavation discovered its very probable real existence. The poems in this collection are all about losing home, losing cities, and then finding out that they were not myths, but real.

TABLE OF CONTENTS

TARTESSOS

OTHER CITIES

ACKNOWLEDGEMENTS

"Etymology of the Living and the Dead" appeared, in an earlier form, in *Cold Mountain Review*.

'Quick" appeared in *GRAIN: The Journal of Eclectic Writing*.

Deepest thanks to Gabrielle David, Kathleen Ellis, and Fred Marchant. And thanks always to Mark, for cooking Greek food, and sustaining a household in which poems can be written. ✺

PREFACE

WINTERS ARE HARD FOR ME TO SURVIVE: I mean this almost literally, as so often I will come down with pneumonia in winter, or trip and fall, or drive badly and get in a fender-bender. Last winter, my grandmother, my father's mother, from whom I was mostly estranged, died at age one-hundred-and-one. I was her namesake. Objects began to arrive in my house — stray odd items, not valuable but in surprisingly large number, willed to me by this woman whom I could not much forgive, and whom I deeply mourned.

Amidst these arrivals, I began to think of the small town in Georgia where she died, and this made me think of many other cities, places that seem almost to have been drowned by history, and then to have resurfaced. While I am not from Andalusia, Federico García Lorca was my first and truest poetry love, and emulating his style of *cante jondo* is always my goal in writing. So, *Tartessos*, the lost city on the Guadalquivir, is the title of this collection of poems. The poems are elegies for cities, and for people, not just my namesake but also other people, named and not named in the poems. It is a book of elegies—for cities where I have drifted, and for people I cannot forget, for worse and for better. In particular, the poet and peace activist Henry Braun I commemorate here, if not with specific poems yet with the idea, which runs through all my work because of Henry, of refusing to be a docile subject, refusing to complacently accept the world's evils.

Tartessos is a city that drowned, leaving a record in myth, and archeology. In these poems, I am not only mourning the dead but also seeking paths of survival. A friend, Mr. D'Silva, happened to share his obsession with megaliths with me during the writing of these poems, and so the poems take on that urge — to find the traces left by people, who are mostly erased — that Mr. D'Silva expresses in his search for ancient architectural forms. Architecture and archeology, those sound like scholarly words, but these poems speak from the heart, sounding out the places left for words in our world. The diasporic, exilic condition of the twenty-first century, when so many people are displaced, is the situation that I address in these poems. If the idiom of the poems is personal, the problem — of lost cities or people who have lost their cities — is all too common these days. Even so, as another winter's arrival is ever so slightly suggested by August's shortening days, I hope that these poems suggest ways to navigate winter's terrain. ☼

— Claire Millikin
Owls Head, Maine
August 2015

INTRODUCTION

IN "SHADOW PLAY," ONE OF THE many extraordinary poems in *Tartessos and Other Cities*, Claire Millikin outlines where we are going in this book. "We will go down," she writes, "into the slant light of our souls," and we will see "under the dirt horizon, solum, / this stain of time, sima, shadow." Lines as strong and deft as these call out for more than a moment of the reader's thoughts and feelings in response. One thinks for instance of Emily Dickinson's slant of light, the one that oppresses us with heavenly hurt and makes a difference down deep where the meanings are, how the landscape holds its breath when it arrives, and how when it leaves that light is like the distance — the pure otherness — in the open eyes of the dead. One thinks also of the other kinds of literary journeys into the under-earth, Dante's journey into the pit of hell for instance. One thinks also of the beachside pit Odysseus digs, the way he performs his rituals and thereby opens an aperture in which he can witness the dead come forth to speak with him.

And beyond literary antecedents, one senses in these lines and this book as a whole an ongoing and relentless descent into the deepest parts of mind. We are going to go below every consoling and seemingly stable surface we know. We are going to probe beyond the "dirt horizon" and into those strange layers of being that are connoted by those interesting geological words "solum" and "sima." We are indeed going on a journey into the shadow land of being, where the specimens we find will need, if we are to be at all précis, some words we've hardly ever used. The past will not be so much a foreign country, but a myth of a lost city, that if we search as long and hard as these poems do will prove to be true, perhaps worse or more unbearable than we can allow ourselves to remember, but real nonetheless. Something like the city of Tartessos, once thought to be merely a mythical trading port on the Guadalquivir River in Andalusia, a city that more recent excavations have shown to have actually existed. As Millikin says in her opening note: this is a book of poems about losing cities, and how losing them turns out to be a way of re-discovering and recovering them as real.

But what are those "other cities"? There are some cities of the poet's adulthood, the places in which she wanders, works, loves, has children of our her own. But then there is another city she carries within. To call it the city of childhood is to make it sound too innocent. It is more accurately called the city of what seems or feels to be childhood trauma. I say "seems or feels" not to dodge the question, but to give a sense of the way these poems glance off this subject, how the trauma appears and disappears, how it need not be the central or the most visible "event" of a given poem, but like that slant of light nonetheless colors and shades everything it touches.

I also want to say that this book does not compose itself into a clinical study in verse, nor is it simply a victim's complaint. Without a doubt there is a deep, barely speakable wound, an atrocity and the recoil from atrocity driving these poems. The reader senses the deepest bonds of trust have been violated early on. And one feels the terrible never-ending present-tense of the wound, the way the memory of it is always fresh, and ready to intrude. But there is something more at work in these poems than the dialectic and dynamics of trauma, something that perhaps artistic practice alone is able to accomplish.

Seamus Heaney, in his essay "The Redress of Poetry," argued for the value of poetry that responds to the unacceptable and horrific aspects of experience. He said that if our experience is at times a labyrinth, "its impassability can still be countered by the poet's imagining some equivalent of the labyrinth and presenting himself and us with a vivid experience of it." That constructed image of the experiential labyrinth thereby offers the mind a chance, in Heaney's words, "to recognize its predicaments, foreknow its capacities, and rehearse its comebacks." Something on that order is what Claire Millikin offers us in these poems. There is at times a maze-like feel to the book, and to feel lost in a maze can be as fearsome as it is bewildering. But throughout this book, you'll find there is also a deep and abiding desire to map the terrain. The poet wants to find her way through the maze, and in the process, she takes us with her, giving us some emotional and spiritual coordinates to help us in our own labyrinths. In "Map of the Night," Millikin tells us:

> a map is an internal thing
> written in the mind, where it must be
>
> to find the way, because dusk in winter blurs
> so far you cannot see.

A map alone does not solve our problems, heal our wounds, or save our souls. But it gives us a chance to find our way, and that is the deepest, most humane lesson in this wise, artful, and deeply moving collection of poems. ✿

— Fred Marchant
author of *The Looking House* (2009)

TARTESSOS

Light Writer

In the city for a little while I had a job describing light.
My duty to write down every fragment, each frame
as light shifted on stairs, in buildings, between the hallways of trees,
in almost sapped avenues that led to defunct shops,
gorgeous tributaries of a polluted river.

What gets broken can be mended through light.
Only the effort to write every detail begins to wear thin
the soles of your palms, as if you had to walk upside down
to remark shadows perpendicular, without rain,
gracile folds of light in low winds.

Sometimes the light was a storm blurring the least echo of men's
legs, feet, hands.
Quickly, I jotted the angles,
got right the curves and lines, light's edges,
but the stuttered substance of light itself eluded me,
until I realized the trick of throwing in myself, my own hand, wrist,
template of flesh
that light cannot go through except by violence.

At first my facility made the work
ecstatic, then I couldn't get back inside myself, couldn't stop
making notes for every shift,
every corner of every street—
to coin the delicate emptiness
of her name by shadows

through which sky moved, circumflex.
I drew deftly every map
reduced to light and got paid for it, of course.
But the money burned in my mouth,
vocabulary erratic and too pure. The room I rented stood quiet,
as if a fire had passed through it.

Party Girls

Climb the night steps to boys,
a low sulfur light along the quay,
boys move toward and away.

Almost an instrument, the rain
makes its white noise,
climb slowly,
the steps slick with freeze.

The small library where you slipped words
under a threshold,
and caught a way to open the door, vanishes.

In winter the house and buildings get so cold
from that openness,
but you could sleep there, safest
farthest from home.

Claire Millikin

The Apportioning of Blame for Girls

i

In the café where we bent to tables,
a homeless woman separated
girls into three categories:

pretty girls, tough girls, and *girls with snakes in their bellies,*
pointing at the girls, assigning the terms.
Vulnerable to light and history, the body bends

for dresses in discarded shopping bags.
So she carried her possessions.
How fragile the world of touch

pretty girl will burn in hell,
she'd declare when she saw me.
The point of rain is shadow first, then indelible thirst,

and so we found a table in the World Café,
the boy from Sarajevo and I, smoking cigarettes,
his wife and infant child left behind.

ii

Find homelessness by degrees, skate, coast
in colder cafés, losing mathematics, a girl
once so quick with numbers.

The homeless woman
was named Aziza
which being translated means *respected.*

She did not see me as her kin,
but at night when I laid down the truth spun
and I found the edge

of eastern seaboard city
where she also slept summer nights, near the World Café
in boxes. The boy and I fell

into a kind of stunned love,
the war over
I learned that season how to eat just enough

not to die, thin wrists, immaterial flesh.
Coast in cafés paying just enough
not to be removed from the table.

The boy from Sarajevo shared with me his cigarettes
and bought for me coffee in cups large as bowls.
At night, sometimes, I'd sleep beneath him.

If the soul empties there is a box waiting,
a box of rain which being translated means *respected*
at the table of the World Café.

iii
She knew the true story
but could only tell it through repetitions
at the rim of sense or sky.

The dead were already buried in his country
by the time we smoked his cigarettes,
and pressed our bodies to the line.

Leaving Tifton

At 5 o'clock in the evening my grandmother is leaving her house.
She takes with her some charred meat for hunger, a kitchen towel
for cleanliness,
and her most expensive pairs of shoes.

After her man died she slept in the bed beside
all her shoes: she gathered those shoes to her body,
shoes, with their vantage of distance,
ballast as she went back down
into impossible sleep that is not death.

So also I have seen mirrored
in my face another face, another back
down the bones of rain.
It is evening, 5 o'clock, grandmother is leaving

her house, for the last time, at five o'clock in winter,
post oak and slash pine ache into shadow
until they become indistinguishable from shadow.

It will hurt to tell the story
but the story is all there is,
words settling

fly ash on severe trees
poisonous coal-fire burning,
and the piano played by a stranger, music carried heavily
on the backs of her slender daughters.

It is 5 o'clock and she is leaving her house
for the last time. Delicately settles
fly-ash from coal fires of another century
for the last time she closes the door
but it will not lock

for already the door is sky
blue transitus estuary,

and I have fallen and broken my knees,
I have fallen
to the depth, the place to tell the story.

Chalk voices of men cross the deepening
sky into apostolic trees.
It is evening and my father's mother disappears
from human places.

A Parable of Trees

i

Grandfather made furniture with his hands
and his wife settled the pieces, *mise en scène.*

All my life, I am trying to speak
a language hewn and precise

but the violence that is part of the trees
echoes in my words.

Anyone can hear the broken trees in my voice.
The wildness of light is in the trees, in their substance.

The substance of a house is nothing
but a tree cut apart—

more subtle than rain or time
more tenacious and real than time

night comes through the forest.

ii

Still the trees harbor this near
possibility of house. House is a dangerous idea.

Grandfather is not waiting
in the house he built with his hands,

his wife's possessions also dissipated, divvied out
beyond the town's vacant shopping mall.

In the trees waits no house
but always the illusion of the possible

house where he is kneeling to his work, lathe and plane.
Every day it must be built again.

I am in that restaurant
waiting under the canopy of slash pines,

homeless, almost,
begging so this man will take me to his house,

where in his childhood bed
sex will stop my name.

Claire Millikin

Shape Notes

At night coming home into Georgia behind
your parents driving you were not asleep,
and those fields reached all the way to Florida, to the gulfs
by curved rivers.

Father and mother would begin, late, to sing
hymns in shape
notes, their voices only then
in harmony, rising in the dark car.

Stay awake, a man without a home
is walking along the sidewalk of another
western Georgia town

it is snowing lightly, at the end
of the 1970s
pale and psaltic trees beyond the town
gather stars, as in a parable of vanishing,

where western Georgia's winter night immense and without flight
listens. Fugitive
begging a place to sleep, something to eat.

The Etymology of Kudzu

Imported for ground cover along train lines
this aching cloud
grandmother discards
from her purse, empty pale ochre

sunset, so I inherit weeds for words.
Kudzu that kills the trees also tangibly
aches so light thickens, transformed,
such aoristic lineage,

to hold the earth around train track banks
while the train shudders in steel harness—
to hold the earth by human names—
rut of knowledge.

Kudzu looks gentle, voluptuous, and we have nowhere else to go
but back. Ground cover gone amuck

like a school where the children cannot stop learning new languages
and so babble untranslatable, charismatic. Its leaves shimmer end-
less vowels.
Kudzu, of what realm
ghosts shape.

The billboards of the descending Carolinas glimmer, late
winter, the windows
of the trees
have emptied.

My love, we are scarred
by what holds us together, smoke—

As if at that station our parents waited yet
new and never ruined, heading north,
the pearl between them.

Claire Millikin

On not eating at McDonald's, circa 1978

The long drive back from Tifton, Georgia,
we would never lunch at McDonald's, the devil's
workshop; but instead eat by the side of the road
foods she carefully packed, in tinfoil.

By late afternoon exhausted
father would relent, buy one cup of coffee
and we would huddle to the dusk table ashamed
to buy nothing more, our hands shining with warmth
as he drank the coffee and we watched.

To be saved takes all you've got,
give up the other stories, pretty girl, this a priori loss.
All my childhood we drove back and forth to western Georgia
county of killed Muscogee,
kudzu folding eroded banks, holding on
to the curved dark space

of salvation,
in no land for never home. In night's starred rain
settle at the delicate table of McDonald's
shaped of Formica and windows so sibilantly dispossessed, rain

rising and sinking in waves. Kudzu is a ghost.
Ever into the vanishing car
this lateral light, relict
flashes
without mercy.

Steles of Tifton Georgia

i

For the brief time I was a user, I became enamored of mirrors—
because you cannot quit the thing
until you go all the way in,
to see in the mirror your bones the ancestors gave,
leaf and line—disavowed

ancient history
of Tifton, Georgia
that my parents never admit,
nothing but rain and burial, else
concerning which they keep quiet.

What use are steles,
effigies, deeper
than the shadow of the elevated highway
I crossed on foot after the car broke down, crossing
to hop a train without a ticket, ride back down
south where a boy waited

at 3 am, to pay my way,
and push me beneath him in the narrow bed
while his friends listened through thin walls.

ii

For what use are the dead
sarcophagi, stele, mirrors—

when using, I'd watch myself in thews of glass in basements
beneath houses, and know
this glass ghost
rising into body,

in bathrooms and hallways, hypogeal.

Claire Millikin

iii

Translate now
from Persian, Urdu, Muskogean, another tongue,
rain's transient mirror,

dead white grass in glistering winter aspect.
In those brief years when I used
it was mirrors I did it for and mirrors
that pulled me through —
to see the family bones,
to see the end and the beginning,
translate
across lexicons for frieze,
how little the word matters, how it is every thing

Attic Bathroom in Tifton Georgia

At last you will have no choice but to bring your wounds there,
your hands folded as in prayer,
bring fractured knees you fell down on
and scraped palms and banged elbows, your bruised breasts,
even the harms of childbirth you will bring,
vestiges of rain arrayed in glass:

for the bathroom left upstairs in Tifton, Georgia, is most
    commodious for wounds
and you will go there despite that other families now own the house,
your own bruised and buried in its eastern graveyard,

in minted stain
their bodies folded beneath their names
the living gone, but the dead remain.

To the attic bathroom of Tifton, Georgia, bring your wounds.
The way your father touched you
ruined the house
but the trees persist and the walls at edges

shadow
time and distance,
no other corridor surpasses
the silt light, eluvium

what the wind has blown
is done.

His father returned wounded from the war
and built a formal place,
the family's first house,
built a cupboard with bandages
and no one, since then, has removed the farthest deepest bandages,
not since 1947.

Claire Millikin

The Sacrifice

Working in the dining hall at vespers,
Keep watch at windows.
What will go deeper than rain shaken from the shoulders
of dying elms, odyl

of wood or forest,
unguarded of late,

the stripped trees wear the stress of light, indelible marks,
slip of the knife
or tongue.
For what has been done in the name of the animals

burned outside the camp. Eleison,
wild deer nosing the boundary,
the hem of evening.

Methodist Mathematics

i

John Wesley, founder of Methodism, kept a log
of all his sins, writing in code:
to each typical sin
greed, lust, dreams of fornication
he assigned a number. For example
desiring wealth and a neighbor's tender daughter
might look like 2, 7, so transcribed.

At evening, I will be walking
back and forth
before grocery stores where I can't afford to purchase.
But anything to try against hunger,
walking, singing, even silent
prayer
even numbers, for a short while,
will ease hunger. By force
the early Methodists converted
speakers of Muskogean.

ii

In mathematics
a function works always the same way, it doesn't veer
no matter what one puts through the machine.

Open the book of geometry and the stars fold and shake, fremitus
this body you have broken
this body of sin.

In the city it will be night when I find her, shadow clock
pews that resemble the ocean
rhythmic fold
to scrim.

Claire Millikin

John Wesley founder of Methodism kept a log
of all his sins, writing in code.
To each sin
he assigned a number
so that none but God could know
the factorable evils, aliquot.

iii

We rented a small house at the edge of tobacco fields,
and walked each day around the outskirts
searching for caporal. We were raised Methodist.

Write down every sin,
now it is winter
the leaves of rain open inward.

When he opened the book of stars and numbers the sky stirred
a narrow inland path.

iv

It will be evening in the church,
rain outside stirring in small curves.
My mother was always soloist
her coloratura soprano rising.

Ride the wave, give in.
Unsteadily, his weight already impressed
against me
by the code of shadow, numberless
that traces flesh.

Shadow Numbers

In heavy rain, the water clock will not work—
rain and night shut its pulse,

useless for tracing time.
Touch the folds of ocean's surplice—

how dark it must get before the room empties
entirely of moonlight

in the basement of a house in North Carolina
listening to other girls laugh, embarrassed of nakedness.

Against nakedness
I have sought the cover of men, where rain begins

and cannot be interpreted.

Circumflex of time. Always, I was quick at mathematics,
but in heavy rain numbers vanish

into the East river, swelling also the Haw and the Eno.
In heavy rain the clock cannot be read—

marking time, the Guadalquivir, the Colorado.
Scapewheels,

the houses we rented kept falling apart—
core where there is nothing but time
running down its engine.

Claire Millikin

7 years I worked in restaurants

A form of exile, to bring food to men at night,
handing them my lost city—

Tartessos Tartessos, did it exist, and was it
a river, a town, or a language?

Tartessos
vanished into the Guadalquivir.

Like the horses my cousin once led to me,
their silken pelage, the broken place of the world

through which the horses walked,
their forms shaped in bronze—

not peril, sword, sky, dominions, nor principalities
bent Tartessos, only

water, that is a form of time.
I have swallowed too much time.

Tartessos disappeared
when the men of lead arrived,

and led the horses beneath trees.
Each night I rode home with him, folded

into the cusp of his arm and we'd pretend
the rain was a forest.

He counted coins in my pockets,
bruised by his weight. Tartessos vanished

into water by another name,
in Spain's only navigable river.

Child's Shoe

In winter I take a wrong turn
and trip splayed onto the graveyard path.

A child's shoe left on the curb, and whose,
casting its late afternoon winter shadow.

I ditch onto my chest so the breath goes flat.
It is always winter when I take a wrong turn,

the Titian light delicate, belying violence.
Early, I learned the way to fall—which parts

of my body to trash, which to save going down—
even so the shoe casts its small shadow

divot, a short curve of depth,
not so much lost as misplaced, a misstep.

Romans kept the dead buried at roadsides, not to forget them.
But my father's mother, my namesake, is buried where I fell.

In the quietness of a photo booth,
I once held the baby and soothed his teeth,

always bought his clothes too large
that they might last

beyond me.

Claire Millikin

Gasoline & Kerosene

We lived down the street from where they sold gasoline,
   and kerosene.
Not a gas station exactly but a dispensary, hydrocarbons
   in metal gallons,
a cinder block structure at the corner of tobacco fields.
Rain also gathered in the branches of the trees.

The street drew a straight line, taking winter to the house.
We practiced vanish and return, call and response. Tobacco
folded up and the roads sank into sky, leaves into ice.
We played chess

at the boundary of day and night
our bodies nearly invisible to each other
fields touching deeper registers, one corner
where they stowed volatile oil beneath earth.

Owls moved in the fields
their voices almost human, that cry
of soul. Nights we shut the doors
and turned up the kerosene heater
its fumes giving us strange dreams.

When Orpheus led Eurydice, at first
it wasn't a serious thing, he led her lightly.
But the gray light as he reached the opening of earth shone
   in his hands
and he couldn't cover his voice
quickly enough not to call for her.

From our borrowed house led a stone wall
that sky moved through rough.
Empty places between stones,

I used to try to build back after rains
kneeling and lifting, strong for a girl.

Eurydice didn't follow him, it was the light she looked for
over his shoulders the luminous unfolding star.
By then
she had already lived in the world of the dead
and knew what it is to have your voice stripped
and given to the owls.

Each night, we had to stop for kerosene,
for warmth, returning home.
When Orpheus turned, it wasn't to test her
it was the way you can think you are done
with suffering, you've gotten clear,
but suffering is never over.

The house in winter schooled us
our cold days at chess,
the game's immutable parallels.
Strong for a girl,
I went down and came back

and walked through the fields. It was Orpheus who vanished.
I don't know where he went, covering with his hands his face
floating in the Haw River past tobacco fields
until his voice becomes my voice
and we are intermingled,
in the desolate winter
craft I practice, faithful yet.

Courtyard Haircuts

It used to be a way to cure depression, getting my hair cut.
I went twice a month, then once a week, then every other day
to the guy with scissors, facing
a snowy courtyard.

Maps once were scrolls
long drawings of a journey remembered
painted down tree by tree, courtyard by courtyard
snow by snow.

The man who cut my hair rarely talked.
There is no real map
for what gets taken away.

Birds took the shorn hair away
and made of it nests, dark shining hair,
black as my mother's.

I assumed he was gay
but once he stroked my hair and wept
and told me he had found at last
a woman with my name to marry.

To cure depression, cut off
what you have been.

Any injury is worth it
but hair is easiest

and when he presses you under him, broken
machine, do not turn from him.

Before the mirror he cut until my face emerged, almost my mother's
under the fleeting shadows of birds.

In me, my father's touch
indivisible as iron and rust.

Haircuts

i

I used to live from accident to accident,
slipped inheritance
of this unstable earth.

We lived by an alley of willows,
drowned golden leaves milked down,

swooping telephone lines,
wires that carry souls
by a thousand cries.

Falling begins to take its toll.

ii

In the courtyard where he cut my hair
red birds drew shadows
down my shoulders,
for my sisters broke me and tore my wings.

And the birds carried the shorn hair for their nests.
He cut my hair so delicately
barely changing the line
that I had to return every week for new work

and when he fathered a daughter
he named her for me.
Copulate, of white birds casting their shadows.

iii

I cut everything away
falling in the graveyard when they buried
my namesake, father's mother,

hitting the earth so hard
I could taste the trees in my eyes.

iv
To get a haircut is to be shriven.
but what's disposed of —
the names of daughters.

Megaliths of Tifton, Georgia

The first houses were tombs—
stone passages—

Portals, dolmens, of domicile
what lasts?

He passes his hands along my face
nothing has been damaged
but this mirror is only a temporary stele,
for grass gets covered by rain.

Winter led the sky from our eyes;

The first sky was stony
having no oxygen,
and no oxygen meant no iron, hematite, or blood.

The first houses were dolmens
they gathered stones for the dead—

and the way stones cast shadows
shaped the first house,
a bruise.
A starred blue leaf
keeping time inside it.

With the maroon coat of my sister inside the door
on the hook, our house persists. From Hall Avenue
cars cast quick lights, ghosts.

Megalith at Willow Drive

Salix, willow that eases pain,
the house cheaply built:
when men visited I stood at the door and took their scarves.

The first houses were megaliths, graves,
and inside them,
illative, a knowledge of distance
beneath the snow in men's eyes.

I think it's over but late at night they still come for me
cast by the foyer mirror.
A mirror is a kind of stele
just more quickly traced.

On Willow Drive, willows kneel into snow
and it is my job to carry the snow
from the well of bad dreams
at which my family still drinks.

As it was my job to please the men who waited late
just to touch a girl like that,
softly on the cheek, nothing less.

The first house was a shadow cast
by stones and the idea of walls
took hold
emerging from shadow's swell.

How softly they will reach,
their coats slipping down into your arms,
the willows drinking
from a well filled only with snow, snow's elisions.

A house is a guise, a stony mask,
even so my sisters blame me for being chosen.

Claire Millikin

Noh Masks of North Carolina

i

The masks separate women
into several types—the perfect beauty, the working girl,
the aristocrat, the mother, the mystical ghost—to list a few.

I grew up in bookstores, kneeling
at my father's feet as he chose.

The beauty of a mask is what it takes away
for I will no longer carry or perform
this story of his touch
how he reached for me and broke the leaves
of shadow so nothing knit back.

From the fourteenth century
onward Noh masks became mystical, neutral.

Putting on the mask, the actor becomes the mask
always a man inside
because a woman has no interior.

The perfect beauty is watching the tragedy—

ii

It is best—when performing—to leave some of one's own face visible
flower of winter
oaks and hickory stiffening
in freezing rain.

Putting on the mask I become the mask
inherited, after all, not a card to be traded
cheekbones, eyes, soul.

Its eye holes small so I cannot see well, precocious.
My father no longer reads but only longs
for a young daughter to warm him.

iii
Put on the mask, the dead return.
The emptiness of masks is the same

as sky behind freezing rain,
scars of theater.

Claire Millikin

Shadow-play

When I was an infant father took me to watch
shadow puppets
and I wept
to see the play which is always good fighting evil
when shown by shadow.

A small girl weeping,
so the puppeteers took me behind the screen to touch
each puppet, thin light golden wood—
see, little daughter, it is nothing
real, only shadow—

father tracing his finger down my clavicle
how vulnerable the collar
of time.
We will go down
into the slant light of our souls
how under the dirt horizon, solum,
this stain of time, sima, shadow.

I have lost at cards despite precocious
mathematical ability,
pressed beneath him
as beneath the line of horizon stays dusk, azimuth,
when rain moves heavily. Just last week

I visited my father's empty house
and on the walls the shadow puppets hung
gold and vermilion paint,
heaven and earth, how will I survive
good and evil.

The puppets reflecting in rain mirrored windows,
all brought back to America after the war.
See little daughter, only shadow.

The Lease

In snow's blue admixture
she walked us through the winter city, into rooms with fireplaces
sealed in endless estivation —
hypogeal, subnivean,
beneath us the subways parsing time and snow,
their ceaseless dreaming buried cwm.

As winter drew tighter around my coat,
dragging through the city
furniture found on street corners,
I kept

carrying the child as if he were my heart,
before grocery stores lit like fires in winter,
flint and the spelled
spall of chipped homecoming.

For Diamonds

In childhood my boyfriend gave me a cross

with a diamond in its center. At that age
I ran ten miles daily, and so the cross slipped
back and forth across my chest
as I ran stride on stride,

the culet digging into my chest
a meniscus, thin elliptical scar

exergue, ghost
around the edges
of my words,
indelible mark of his cross.

The farther I ran
the deeper it worked,
diamond cut. I never wanted breasts.

The Other Myth of Delphi

We moved frequently in those days without fate
apartments entered empty, left empty.

Fate is a clean thing, winnow
down the options by pretending

that your father will not show up at the door
of the last apartment asking

for his only daughter, precious thing
kept secret, beneath his shadow the white

gingko shimmering with sleet.
To keep ahead of fate takes all you've got

decades pass
and still you have not confessed your name

was also your father's mother's
and how you are broken

inside helps you keep apartments so clean, no one can see
they are inhabited, Quickly the reivers

strip fields pale with harvest.
The other myth—that the oracle could not say it

that she stuttered and could not speak
that words failed her and the fields sank

down from the omphalos, the world's navel
where the meaning of second birth is not beautiful

and empty apartments shine bright on winter's lam,
rooms that are not ours filling with light, golden

eagles calling in arcs. However,
his family left that country a generation back.

Claire Millikin

Salvaged Dog

I was not harbored as a child. Hunting
through shellac, mother wept
playing the piano
in her acetate nightgown.

She used to buy me every year a new
nightgown, just like hers and sizes smaller, saying wear nothing
underneath. That nakedness still haunts me,
the note I cannot play.

Even now, the dog sleeps
under the shadow of my story—
how ever will I trace that music—
beneath trees cut down

ever since the 1970s, a thousand times a thousand
forests folded shut.

She is playing the piano,
and it could save my eternal soul
to give up, to walk away
but I cannot stop

the gap of light that opens
late dusk before the shopping mall,
to swallow poisons
but die of shadows.

The Mark

Uncles' cattle herds walked
marked by the family name.
I remember more clearly seeing that name in the ears of cattle
than any other place. The name, how it looked

so burned, my hidden name
singed, folded
under the ear of rain,
of voice. Deeper in the pine forest animals

answer to nothing
human, but they branded the cattle, coffle
of mother's brothers. The broken place
where one is named,
bend of ear—

he will kneel down and stroke your hair
and it will matter, even years later it will matter
that you could not speak
up and say no.

It was a family matter
to be kept private,
as the forest for hunting, this distaff line.
My father had no brothers
but the brothers of my mother,

her flesh transfigured
into male lines, and so at first I trusted
slash pines, borrowed ledgers.
In winter one hears rivers closing.

When asked my family name,
I say nothing—
brand in the ear, the language gate—
my father's favorite.

Claire Millikin

Under the Bed Apartment

The ad said seeking roommate,
gave an address in the best
part of the old city, small doors opened and led
deep, a knock answered by slippered feet,
along gleaming hallway, I've come about the room

oh yes, the last boy
didn't work out,

Cold feet
from walking in the winter darkness.

The west of any place is endless,
the west is the place of the dead,
subnivean knowledge,
under the bed.

The Golden Damages

When she packed the furniture to be shipped,
across each piece she taped tight
my name. In a warehouse in snow
the inherited furniture waited,
the tape tightening into the wood by resin

so that when it arrived
years later I could not remove the signs.
I live in a damaged house,
with only the man who drove the furniture

down highways to carry my name.
When I removed the tape, having proven who I was
under the lips
of the furniture deliverer,
I found the furniture ruined by its tags,

scar and weft that tied it to me
by name. Holocene it is still going on.
So I took what was given, dead
white grass through cracks in the steps,

karst beneath river and under forest,
ash in the throat,
a name torn loose.
No one's daughter now.

Claire Millikin

Popcorn

The girl next to me kept a clock
in the back of her locker, its arms shimmering like new rain.

She lived in a trailer outside town with a man
twice her age, Hickory trees' rough turns

shadowed our hands when we sat before it.
Late at night after the clocks

of hickory wound down, her boyfriend would drive us back
swerving in the road, sweven, a dark and formal dream,

we rode past cattle and leaves pressed indigo,
he'd veer, high, but get us

safely to the not-house where she'd cook popcorn, indigenous
to the Americas, from Mesoamerica by violence it came north.

I tested into senior math, at age fourteen, swallowing
almost nothing else in those fast days,

my hands so thin you could see through them, a leaf in autumn,
the lines of fate erased and nothing

to take their place. I will feed you she said the first day
we saw each other standing at the lockers shivering

in sunlight, a caught, bleached place.
For nets of leaves and rain,

the cattle swallow nothing but bad dreams
and she cooks popcorn, the only food I will eat

for it tastes not of substance but of light.
In rain, how luminous and unguarded this house.

Suitcase, Omphalos

There is a hole in the night
into which my grandfather packs a suitcase

and says *hurry*
it is time to leave this country,

where my sister sleeps with her daughter in a small bed
next to an enormous bottle of nail polish remover,

a hole before which I awaken at 2 am and run
my hands along the counter, famished

for a country without a suitcase,
a hole in the night and my grandfather says *it is time*

pack up now.
He buttons shoes and coat, a small man

only the size of the dime
I put in my pocket

for some long delayed telephone call
into the natal country of rain and pine trees.

He dreams of rain
and there is a hole in the night

through which rain falls
where my body is not my body

but only belongs to my son
to whom I gave birth with such suffering

Claire Millikin

the horizon contracted
and I named him for his father's father

in the manner of the Greeks.
A hole in the night where Delphi once waited,

axioms and prophecies:
a ruined unimpressive temple, small round stutter of stones,

a crack in the earth, the side of the mountain for visions,
so much less impressive than the trees

where we wandered in the woods
looking for the button of the world, two stones

carried by two ravens. Here they meet.
So often these days I do not know myself. I mean

there is a hole in the night
through which I address you

with words carried
in the manner of ravens carrying stones.

OTHER CITIES

Parties My Elder Sister Took Me To

The law is a forest, Anne, its tall trees elegant with or without rain,
oak, poplar, even the ruined elm.

What am I but ruined
by the parties to which my elder sister towed me,
killing moonlight on our hands.

The law is a forest, in moonlight
when we come to a house almost empty
but in the cupboard there is tea,
left years before, when the owners disappeared.

Drink from that well
spoiled with moonlight, tasting
this mirror knowledge.

The law is a forest, I wake these nights with the memory of it.
Downstairs the kettle shakes on its fire.

My sister brought me to offer
something pretty, small doors for open eyes.

The law is a forest, Anne, elegantly drawn and if not endless
yet infinite to the mind.

The boys will empty their pockets
their hands tracing cheekbones, eyes.

Always a coin on the table, and sister vanishes to eat
with the women in the kitchen.

The law is a forest but no one gets home through it.
Every version of the story

sounds false but is true, interior,
our coats on the floor.

Stripped forest after rain: a done thing.

Claire Millikin

Map of the Night

Maps once were scrolls
lines to be unrolled,
forests listed tree by tree.

I drove fast enough to shake off
memory but the same scroll followed.

Driving, at dusk, I used to speed, tossing the map;

at dusk speeding gets dangerous.
But a map is an internal thing
written in the mind, where it must be

to find the way, because dusk in winter blurs.
Driving, I used to speed, dangerously at evening

to get home that was never there.
Speeding in the car
is a form of speech

resisting translation
just as bad dreams move so quickly
events folded on each other

in multiple exposure.
For many years I loved my sister enough to lie for her,
raveling the distance.

Cuts

I did not grow up in a mansion,
but after I disappeared,
my mother inherited a broken one.

Her first night, the red steps grew slick with rain
and housewarming guests, slipping, left injured
though most returned.

I too stuck with it, haunting the place,
loving my mother against reason,
her silk dresses in the third-story boudoir, seasoned

with sweat and perfume.
She wanted to erase
the evidence of my childhood,

tabled beneath winter sky,
dark red steps
slick in freezing rain.

Later she glued grit to the steps for traction
but it was too late—vertigo was in me,
wrest of snow.

And the cracked regulator leaked.
Then they turned off the gas,
so ice sank into the thorax of the house.

I'd cut myself to breathe,
the way plants survive
by small apertures, stomata.
And put on long red sleeves.

Claire Millikin

Underwear

An exchange, for something gone
wrest from syllables the wound,

as in childhood mother established the rule
give to the weak from the strong.

And so when the car broke down
she had me strip and give my underwear to my sister

who had none, my skin going blue in the exchange
as winter bent down

long ruins of roadside weeds.
An exchange: how quickly

nakedness becomes wordlessness.
Stand by the roadside and cars and trucks pass like ghosts,

you become the ghost. She has measured your worth,
how strong you are, strong enough

to strip before winter
and survive. The taste of grass and gravel in your eyes

gaze against asphalt, pitch.
Words become light and pulse.

An exchange, for what goes down
rises, we rode to the airport in the back of a stranger's truck

after he stopped and picked us up, hitching.

I will find a plane to catch
and clothes to wear and not take off.

The narrow deer slide into the forest for winter,
oaks casting sciagraphs, marks in faint winter sun.

Tift County, Georgia

That other street,
the one not seen on any television,
where rain has just drawn off
before houses not well kept,
a place where I'd be safe, unseen—

so I ride my bicycle away from fate
and then returns my father's county, by swerve
ineluctable—

young trees open. It's the same story with roses
I should know, grandfather kept them
sprayed heavily with pesticides
that sink into earth

where the chemicals spread and fan, killing everything with a mind.

The young trees open and it is not snowing.
Leaves of paper, tree of night
in the graveyard where I did not make the funeral, prodigal.

Indigo paper once was used to hold blocks of sugar,
then unfolded and re-used to dye clothes;
so deepest dreams are always harsh,
deepest blue—

young trees open and I descend,

the most beautiful face
goes missing

into the pocket of clay and grass.

Only the surface layer
of history passes for truth.

Claire Millikin

Winter Coat

1.

To not have to walk
however many miles
in the far simile of a winter coat
beneath sequent trees, and cars throttling sky
as covering to have the winter coat
so that no one and no snow
rub raw, friction, its umbrage of thickest wool.

A coat is not a house
but may shimmer
with such reasons
wool and weft, I have come back
from another country
and have no coat for snow.

2.

When I moved north, no coat
only the frail pink shift
acetate too fragile
thinner than silk, remnant
from grandmother's closet, thick with her used up
perfume, grass in the sleeves,
from such low shelves of earth,
ebb and rise of voices that are shadows
from that country
where mother and father bought for me
no winter coat
so I arrived in the north, shoulders naked.

3.

And put on the blurred night, a man's coat,
the first I slept with
in that place gave me the football jersey he wore

as a teenager, still several sizes too large
but I haunted its form.

So much of balance
requires walking for miles
after falling
winter coat he put on my shoulders
for such nakedness
as winter carries: a shining
impossible object, cipher.

4.
The blurred light above and below a railway bridge
gets buried into earth,
beneath men's shoulders.

5.
He said, where is your coat?

To own a winter coat, without feathers or with,
sky pipes ice between the trees,
evening's settling glass
of ghosts, birds, scavengers.

I am borrowing again
a winter map stitched
into its lining,
sky into water.

Winter Coat 2
She says I have come from another, warmer country
and have no winter coat;
so cleaning the office buildings she does not
step outside, coatless
into the snow.

After poverty
teeth remember longest
winter without a winter coat.

Winter Coat 3
1. She says she has no winter coat
2. and cleans the buildings staying
3. carefully inside, away from snow
4. for she came from a warm country
5. also when my parents sent me north
6. they bought no coat for me.
7. Naked to have no coat, to the bone.
8. Even the sons of Isaac need such.
9. He said, I will give you my coat.
10. When starving, lanugo covers the body.
11. I give her my coat.

The Pool

To the west of sorghum fields they dug the pool,
painting the interior
a dense and variegated blue
mosaic, tesserated

stones so that sinking we'd come apart,
pulse, voice, breath.

This depth:
at last the net of bad dreams will no longer catch me,
small marks of rain against my thighs.

Water is my element, by birth, ephemeris,
rain's pulse
not intended to drown, serein
slowly, slowly feeding the trees and grass.

But they gouged a gap in earth for the pool,

trees' shadows under the pool's skin,
backward veins,
and father is in me again,
his voice in my name.

Ephebe

My father once had a student whom he loved,
a slender man, almost still a boy.

Aerugo rust of dusk,
down where the fescue grass vanished
into stubble fields.

We lived by fields
that now are streets.

Aleatory, aliquot:
factors of chance.

My father kept in his heart the student and myself,
we'd ride home late at night;
even by well known stars I could not navigate.

The young man could run like a deer,
and then I too learned to run
quickly and got so slender,
I couldn't see or hear. Fine, soft
hair, lanugo, on my shoulders.

So animals in winter almost starving deepen
their keep, turning in one furrow.
My father loved his student, and also me,
but no one survived his desire:

in winter, animals sleep, soft and teleological
the place where sleep drives,
factoring night.

Saltworks

The boys without mothers ride bicycles on ice
in the glittering neighborhoods of childhood—
seedlings
sheltered in gametes of salt.

Behind houses,
the boys slide on ice,
their bikes reflecting
like a room when it's emptied.

The boys without mothers ride bikes on ice
swerving where the highway
unfolds from back roads and it's alright
for a long time, for years, nothing happens

the way you can go all day and not eat or drink
and you feel cold and sure
like a figure reflected by ice.

And then at night
you cannot breathe
for hunger, rhizomes stilled with cold.

Without mothers—
had they vanished into death, divorce, the stories different,
the same marks—
frayed cuffs, raveled trouser hems, a risk,

boys' hands closing on my wrists.

Once I too spoke another language, my mother tongue
not taught me by my mother.

In bad dreams reiteratively I travel
with my parents to arrive
where language ravels,
luggage opening.
How shall I remember my mother tongue,
empty house of her voice. Listen,

how fast a bike goes
when you ride it downhill on ice.

The Bicycles

They are not polished or oiled
the way vowels within words slide.
They stutter with time.

I could be riding down any road
but it is always the same town.

Bicycles swerve where the street gives out
to gutter and a slur of polluted water
that looks like milk.

Mother's milk, lead, arsenic.
The bicycles are dangerous—of course!
They get going so fast.

Riding in my father's lap, once, my foot draped
and caught in spokes, half
torn-off before I spoke of it. Speak

so that even the sky I have swallowed
will have done no harm
and sleep will come
as hickory trees vanish into shadows,
just past the edge,

the house I can never reach, bicycles shining,
spokes and wheels—
riding is infinite, cash out
all the bad deals accepted on the way.

Claire Millikin

The Salt Meals

In the city we went seeking bowls of salt
to sustain us inside
winter in crowded rooms.

For salt resists shadow,
its delicate particles cast only the faintest shallows,
rising and sinking the city's fossil shells

beneath fields. The taxis
move into snow
like doors,
axis framing night's interiors,

a psalm for salt,
even so I would dissemble time, for
how do I reach the essence, the gist of that loss?

Trees filling with snow that is no shelter
a cold ulterior mirror, salt,

a psalm to bind the wound.

Heidegger

for Roxana Trujillo

In the evenings, after waiting tables, I wrote an almost endless
treatise, making very little sense,
in response to Martin Heidegger's theory of thrown-ness.

Each time I walked into the closet
of his language I found there my elder sister's golden shoes,
worn-out, discarded after too many dances.

To whom does Martin Heidegger refer? Who is thrown?
I turned his words through doubly washed hands
begging for pardon.

You will walk into a clearing
in the forest where words emerge

from slant of trees, slash pine, sawgrass, vermilion
edge of day ending, this cant ellipse of light.

In a derelict house boys had their fêtes
and they took me in for my face, misreading the bones.
You know, Heidegger was something of a cheat,

and also a telephone
cheats the voice it carries through the forest
a singed place, a clearing amid high tension wires.

If I followed the tracks of deer
it would return me to the outskirts
of the same restaurant where I once worked,

thrown out—vegetables, coffee grounds, kudzu.
I kept it spare
the years I waited tables,

and it was hard to think clearly eating so little.
Words emerge by singe,
the deer breath tight

at human doors.
In the evenings, after waiting tables, I returned to Heidegger,
a desk set by the closet

of my vanished sister's golden bedroom. In a rainstorm
once when she was driving
I held on beside her,

so tight a skin, without shelter.
Years later, I was invited
to read what I'd written on Heidegger,

in the company of a philosopher
who asked me
to lay my head on his lap.

Of Grace and Gold

For years, I was mystically clumsy, falling down
hard, fracturing knees, hands.

When his mother died, I inherited all
the damaged pieces,
what no one claimed,
gaudily and cheaply reupholstered.

Lay across the wound
words
that won't get at
what it means to fall.

Mystically abrupt, premorse,
all the ways I tried to cheat
this downward depth

how golden the latches of gingko.
I applied every lie
my teeth going bad

with sweetness, thrown at the curb of any apartment,

perimeter,
alluvial drift.

The house of small objects

Homunculus in the house of small objects
shift of shadowed grass:

this house shrinks music and sky
that must fit at last into the boxes
of eyes, as light into words.

At evening's crux everyone still out is lost.
Gather for the house of small objects
the pearls of dancing rain.

among the mint's
soft dense pellage.

Fold the paper into wings,
now fold the wings into notes. We opened
windows to smoke in the apartment,
to leave intact the corridors of evening—

coins of psalms fit in palms:
at evening our hands are small.

Corner Pizza Joint

When it was almost over, the storm, pulling away
rope shadows of rain,
my father took me to the corner restaurant,
fed me salt. Gold taxis shifted and vanished,

metamorphosis,
carry your father like a cross
his hands on your breasts.

Davit, set down the boats
for rescue in such shining taxis,
summer and the rain's sudden shutting—
telluric—taxis move quickly and vanish.

He doesn't have to say a word,

It was also my country,
I lived there, but slept rough,
staying awake to trace the taxonomic shadows,
for such distance between shadow and water,
as childhood turns, vanishes
after heavy storm.

The Pianos

In several myths and religions the deity is blind
—either his eyes are pierced
or his side, or it is just the ruined
world he has created

that forces him to turn away. Easily
I could stutter at the piano
for notes are numbers
that came naturally to me

and no one measured the gift.
But when I needed somewhere to sleep
it was waiting—
boys at the bridge, piano-dark curve,

bright and dry translucent leaves.
A leaf-scar,
through the tree's wound
its voice emerges

always flawed.
In the music building
after another night in the ruins,
I could hear them, soul by soul, the players playing on.

Take any man's offer, to enter sleep

by no other door,
by rain on blue branches.

Moths

(for Joan Braun)

No other voice is so drawn by light.
Bring through this country of winters
spent trees and impotent factories
the filaments of moths,

their wings trapezoids bisected by shadow,
for they descend
down into the vineyard

as on the bus when I was 13
the driver asked for my hand, saying
this is the most beautiful
you will ever be

was there no harm? grapes with their thin and fragile skin
enfold rain
so also tightens a dark and pure reservoir
beneath curtilage, hypogeal, around and beneath the moth.

Early I got taken—
In summer, ride the subway,
for who will reassemble the blessing,
knowing all that is written is written in the names of moths.

When grandfather died, his wife, my father's
mother, put all the shoes she owned
in the bed by her side, for a ballast.

I walk endlessly by the side of moths
for the truth is in them.
My shoes wear thin.

Claire Millikin

Moths float, souls released.

From the train I am riding into the Bronx
into light, emerge the moths
and I will be forgiven,

as buildings rise
in nets of rain.

The Vow

In the neighborhood of my infancy, the mothers did not tend
their children's hair.
So gradually, as we slept and turned and cried
as snow fell through the fractures
of sky between branches
as we rode our bikes down rough hills
unprepared for human habitation,
our untended hair matted
taking on the twists of time. Small sticks, leaf bits, haulm
we'd shake out the detritus,
still our hair tightened, torsade
a record of gravity
that our mothers made no effort to erase.

They slept through the long afternoons with rain
brushing the cloth of grass and dirt. Hair is a ghost
nothing living
persists like that, a record of each turn in sleep,
and the drawing of curtains and the opening of closets and shoes.

When I grew up, I cut off my hair,
and stopped speaking to my mother,
keeping my hair so short, nothing
could be read from it, Milk and honey.

But the voices gather, choughs in the rough
back courts of soy fields and tobacco
and as hair grows back so also mothers
must empty the closets of daughters who have left.

Hair is a ghost, as Sampson knew.
Our mothers slept through rain's echo,
silt settling in doorways.

Claire Millikin

I never meant to be holy, it came by mistake, first no wine,
then no cutting or brushing of hair, and then no house,
and the boys mistaking me
for something wild
to take down.

Gas Stations

The Archean earth had no oxygen, no blood, no color red.
I sometimes think of this fact that I read,
quickly, over my daughter's shoulder in a science museum.
When driving into gas stations at dusk, look
how tight sky's helm. Oxygen wasn't always a given.

Rocks shoulder the evidence of those millennia without rust
virid, verdigris,
so also the gas station shimmers, bright green fluting.

It is almost a house but no one
can stay home at a gas station: hypogeal
scent, gasoline rising will knock you out,
dangerous to breathe longer than an instant —

hematite, feldspar, karst,
gas stations are for saying good-bye,
my mother's hands move,
breaking apart time and light.

In America, we can drive without stopping
for depth of gasoline untapped,
listing toward the edge.
Maybe rain will fall bringing oxygen and leaves

down into that earliest room, where she is leaning
against the wall
at the city outskirts, lighting up. It's true

I never had a living daughter.
But the museum was real,

In the pocket of my losses, lithic
streaked red evidence, late
sunlight on the dash.

Claire Millikin

Houses of the 1970s

I was born and raised in that country of damage
behind the rains,

Vestigial houses, built of shoddy material
like TV sets. Behind the houses: trampolines
in deepest indigo

where I once learned to fly
shadowed back against earth,

unfolded cranes.
The houses of the 1970s built quick and cheap, for television

families who watched the screen endlessly,
back stairways to rains
where houses still met forest

the turned river running,
the trampoline a mode of flight, dangerous
for its architecture of spent sky,

and the mothers despondent,
never my own mother.
She slept in the burgundy bedroom with willow shadows

behind the houses,
folds of rain
honeysuckle pressed to gulches,

in puddles oil scrim shined to mirror.
I grew up in houses where no one was careful
not the builders, not the painters, not my father,

who took what he could get.

The History of Water

Men walk deep into the water for only two reasons
to be baptized born again,
or to drown
when there is no other way out.

The evening after they buried my grandmother,
I worked the long shift,
fever coming on with unbearable thirst,
drinking water and serving men
tall glasses of wine.

Men walk into the water, the younger boys
still want a girl like that
but after they buried her I lost heart

working the long shift I began to shake with fever.
Water is not infinite but thirst is.
Men walk into the water

and it is not the river Jordan, because this is America, drown
in the sanctuary shale of the restaurant's long shift,
no one told me of the funeral
I found out by accident. Tintoretto,

greatest painter of the Venetian school, his hands moved
more slowly than water to track the rain
down stained skies, appanage.

In Venice the history of water is all history
a city slowly drowning,
glass of soul—

go under him, go under
for water has an endless history of sinking, and men know
to reach their hands into me,
searching drowning.

Men walk into the water— here is the history
of my grandmother, never painted
by Tintoretto,
she fell into earth and was buried

under her name that is my name.

The Ride

In bad dreams I am still facing a lottery system
by which exactly 12 people receive housing
out of 12,000, leaving the other 11,988 homeless.

My baby sister and I once got lost, walking
down the corner of Griffith Park in Los Angeles,
the year I was a track star and could run so fast
that when I fell my knees shattered. Before that,

we got lost and a woman slowed down
as the rain got harder,
so we got in her car, heads tucked like horses,
and began the ride.

She said she cleaned houses for a living
and never wanted girls to get lost
then she drove us through Los Angeles,

circling in and out of alleys, side streets, a corrugated map of storm
weaving in and out of languages, telling the city's history,
that I knew and my baby sister didn't
and so I knew she was keeping us
safe and trapped, calends

first day of summer, riding out a grief.
I am riding it out, still,
words in translation for the city
angelic and naked, a map is nothing

but a hand traced along the shoulder,
touch, topographical, scars of survival.

We rode in this shimmering storm for hours, a native, she knew
the city like a body.
The hand is the first map, touch.

where she opened the car door, as rain drew off
and we walked a few blocks back
to the temporary apartment,

that last summer I was still a champion
and had no breasts.

Neighborhood Mathematics

Walk late at night shivering hard
breathing against your hands
rain shaping trees and grass in dark sky,
for what might save you is the way forms shift—

squares rotated become octagons, and within octagons circles,
and neighborhood rooms
become sky that disappears through windows.

No census for a family like yours,
mouths open for the ghost.

Between such houses space goes desolate yet
this turn of mathematics, verge still unsolved,
the fathers with their mistresses, or you,
never safe to go back to that room in that house

but all you have wanted is to return—
oaks curved to sky—
what's left, the narrow tables women shoulder afterwards,
bread and salt, doors left ajar to birds.

The Rain Door

By the end of the year I bought a door
to use as a table.

At the door I ate all my meals. And, on the door I laid a notebook,
a pen, a typewriter. At first
I wrote simply to name the objects in the room.

All things waited behind the door;
the door was my city,
through the city I walked to claim my door—
buying it used but clean
from a store that sold old doors, oak

because desperately I needed a way through,
not a table or a desk on which to rest
but a door to go through distance,
an entrance.

The arc of late winter light, canted
into tobacco sheds
that none have used for decades
matched the quietism of my door.

Even if my father used me for a door,
taking me swimming just to see me stripped,
I still learned not to drown,

for the door is a way down
and I knew the way down
its own language—

How still the door waited, laid on its base of stacked bricks

Claire Millikin

I walked through the city to gather
and carried back to plinth the door.

I walked through the city carrying bricks,
a kind of penitent,
shouldering it,
all to set the door parallel to the street,

and my body perpendicular to the door,
ephemeral cross.

Quick

In autumn, solitary confinement,
they asked me to take some tests in mathematics,
to go back to high school on the right track.
In a narrow room they laid before me the papers.
I wasn't a woman yet, at fifteen, too thin to bleed.
My hands opened like clean fans, finger and brin.

I began assessing the numbers.
For three days, the sheets of questions
given to me to solve, beside a luminous window,
by the patient social worker, who'd brought with him his knitting,
his quick fingers through teal wool,
a skein as supple as sky.

With each correct answer I stepped up the stairs
of a narrow escape, above the marred codes of tobacco fields,
their depth of succus, earth in furrows.
Like clean water to drink those numbers,

to lay my empty hands along the pages and gather the right answers.
He was knitting quietly, tenderly
the fields turned into later shadows,
then everything grew late.

Of course the high school could fit me in its advanced mathematics,
and I could begin again as if it had never happened,
the tomb, the cross, the resurrection,
as if I had never left my father's house
to not be touched again, each algorithm
a code, a stain I retrieved, unwinding the tented cloth.

Fish only for men. How well I knew
those kids from juvie, how well I knew
to say nothing when I saw them afterward on the street,
but meet them later along railroad tracks late afternoons,
without mathematics, almost without bodies for our love.

The Peacock

Systaltic hinge
of cry, in their cages held fine
this structural iridescence of peacock feathers, a tilt
so quick the eye hurts.

I remember their destitution:
in the park they were ill fed
and our hunger matched theirs.

We were attracted to them,
drawn to the lure of unseeing.
We walked by the park each evening
scattering bread for our souls, swallowing
hunger, its absolute force.

The peacock's cry settles on my tongue.
Don't you see, the eyes of the peacock see nothing,
desolate for all their splendor,
so also when I fell I was crying out God's name,
Eleison,

a fugitive iridescence so fast it hurts the eyes.
In my father's house I was an open eye,
and willows fanned their wings.

School Bus into Forest

In half light the golden bus
moves by the outskirts of fog gray forest.
Hush of rain slowing,
daughters fold small fingers into books.

So also, I listened to your glistening voice, highest soprano
and built myself from what you cast away.
Beyond the school the Doric forest stretches.
Taxis disappear toward any city.

When the grown-ups smoked in the back yard
we'd sit in the driveway car, windows open to summer,
you always the driver, my elder, without a key—
pretending.

Unseen by men
turn on the radio
of our voices and sing louder than rain
warm and dense in summer's helm.

How is it your father found you, a decade later, in a city apartment
and you had forgotten to eat
for days, weeks, drinking water from the tap,
standing stunned at the sink.

In semi dark, the school bus
pulls into forest, beyond
oneiric traffic. Daughters on the bus read carefully
not moving their lips, piacular, atoning for rain.

By necessary contradiction
your voice rising into my mouth, I listened
and the car went nowhere, of course,
but summer sky came to us, moving through open windows.

Claire Millikin

He found you in the red apartment
your hands on the sink, drinking, a swan to water.

Above the highway the apartment shook like a lantern.
So slender from that fast, he carried you easily as a book.

Listen, the red voice, cannel, burns.

I still have my reasons
for telling the truth.

Etymology of the Living

It was once believed that fire was a living being,
fire consumed what it swallowed,
it moved and had body, and a kind of voice, audible.

And yet fire had only one name
while trees have many—olive, juniper, cypress, pine, to list a few—
so fire was counted as something living
but incompletely named, elusive.

Fire swallowed the skin of earth,
to touch this living thing—fire—
hurt more than any other emergence, phoenix.

Unlike snow fire was always itself:
there could be no category of fire, because burning is burning.
A body of water drowns, if deep enough
and ice also holds still, liminal, between snows,

but fire takes on the depth of the thing it swallows:
black pine and plum knelt to flame.
The trees got named, living and mute but with stories,
beginnings, and endings.

Only fire has no story.
Fire is the end of stories.
And so fire was the first living thing
to be removed from the category of the living.

Quick as lightning, in my father's house opened
fire in which we singed our meat for supper.
I used to believe if I starved myself
long enough it would wither
the history of his touch,
flattened needles of bad luck. Pine

burns fitfully, in resinous cants and sparks.
It was once believed that luck
was a living thing, but fire consumed
red needles, of pine, of juniper, made ember and char.

Fire shakes in ladders of light
and the latches flash;

never allowed to enter, fire, too fiercely human,
is caged in human houses. But I think it is waiting
at this edge,

to ride back, all the dark
engines burning.

The Forms of Night

The true color of night is green
virid and shaking. In some dreams
I retrace a night in Djakarta before
I learned how to speak,
when mother held me like a balance weight
and the protest in the street
turned rough. I felt her shake, like leaves in heavy rain.
In every version of this story, a man will arrive and see her beauty
and say, in English, follow me, lady,
and we walk into the form of night, its green depth
longer and steeper than stars' farrow distance.
Shouldering metal stars
we follow the man who addresses my mother
through corridors of shoulders.
Even if my hands shake, I know the answer,
the real shade of night a harsh outré green,
depth beneath depth.
At some point it will happen: a man will stand before you offering
shelter which could mean anything
death, disappearance, your only chance
for survival. Through the night I become my mother's shadow
a thin rain borrowing her pulse
from the moon's clear heart. I am worn out
by the unequivocal moon.
He took us to a shelter at the western edge of the city,
a house shaped of rain
on tin; steep wind slammed the green door.
I held my mother's hand.
In that language in which I still dream
a hand is a hand, a door a door, night is night.

Evening Rooms

So often at evening rooms
will seem as if they weren't there
and you will be reminded of the first apartment

where your mother left you
and did not return, so that you became an infant
in other women's arms. At evening, rooms will gleam

with afterglow, as if mountains sheltered
instead of recorded a history of violence
so excessive even the shoulders of sky turn away.

At evening rooms shine, lit as if language were nothing
but a brilliant coat to put on:
meridian emblem,

ephemeris set by star.
Instead of a pair of shoes,
the only one left in this house.

Palindrome

My uncle will collect me from the station, drive skirting

the edge of the town, past the fields' canted angles

to the house where wires have caught in the night

and turned to cinder. There is no city, only its edge,

no harvest, only gold premise of what might scythe,

and no house, only the promissory note of loss.

But my uncle, mother's only brother, says *hush*

and mourning doves come on

with the reliquary stuff, and I give up

looking and reaching for the center. There is only the edge.

At evening he collects me from the station, next door

in a house with open windows a woman is singing

the Byzantine scale, in which I was trained

upon marriage, but I decided

to go back, after all

beloved by my uncle, mother's only brother, skirting

canorous fields, candescently emptied

for merest entrance this station.

Claire Millikin

Hiroshima, Mon Amour

It will happen at last, despite my best efforts
to enter the precise
and endless record of rain on my wrists,
I will sit down at evening in a small room,

not an empty room, a room neither beautiful nor outwardly desolate,
holding a glass of water
that catches the light
of my thirst
holding *your death that goes on*
my life that goes on.

The curled tender sugars of the berries
my child gathers from the untended yard
and forgets, in a white cup to rot.
Or are you transposed to the fox's eyes, that tamped fire?

It will happen, some evening when I no longer have work
to finish, I will hold a glass of water
and not be able to drink
for all your unholdable weight.

Only the fox's eyes,
clocks of rain and persistence
guarding an emptied world,
should decide.

Lead

Lead was the first mechanism for printers
malleable, shape the words.
What gets passed on? My mother sleeping in the narrow beds
of other countries before I was born—
small horses of light in our mirrors.

The anchor of a house; lead sinks into the bone and stays,
awaiting starvation to leach outward through calcium into the blood
in pregnancy. My mother slept in narrow beds—
you tell me *it's all an illusion*
but something is damaged within.

The wind moves through midsummer grass
and the windows of the house shake with light.
Mother sends cash
apologizing for the weight
of my father that pressed against me infant nights.

But lead does not dissipate
inspissate spirit it thickens
Et spiritu sanctus the rain in the grass of our names.
And even the sewing rooms of my aunts cannot salvage
the weight of light at evening, as I am in a foreign country again
counting coins, planchets, blanks.

Lead was the first language printed
soluble star of its heft, almost liquid.
Soon I will write in that language that cannot be tarnished or translated.

Thickening beneath boats the ocean rises. Rain moves up the coast—
a letter sent from the unrecoverable place, the sewing room of my
        mother's sisters.

Bird Apparitions

When we were seeking an apartment in the city,
rain monadic and strong
took us through alleys, and corridors.
And, set into doors,
the mirrors of rentals showed back birds —
oriole, swallow, robin, ruby hummingbird —

of which one cannot speak
when dreaming of the nightingale
its tongue cut out, Philomel.

Closer by the ocean, cold gulls soared —
plover, cormorant, osprey, tern.
They'd vanish at doors
but their forms held
reflected in the rentals' mirrors,
sleeves of shadow on the immanent.

Why do tenants always leave mirrors?
Keys exchange rapidly, but mirrors stay
stapled to doors
reflecting and refracting light — *etalon* — a caught circle of shine.

The damage was done —
glass so stapled to doors —
such mirrors cannot be erased.

There is no mother for stories
such as ours. In apartments always up for rent
birds appear in mirrors, grebe, chough, sparrow, killdeer.

Cheap apartments, eloquent
of birds' afterimages —
dove, whippoorwill, raven and kingfisher. Nothing
else we inherit.

Event Horizon

In the days I rented a place behind the shopping mall past the
swamp, *cul de sac* rendered invisible by sprawl, each day I took a
few dollars from the small purse mother had given me on her depar-
ture and spent it on doll furniture.

The apartment otherwise empty, I wanted to re-read the course
of childhood, beginning not with people but objects: dolls in their
silence so mirroring trees, heavy oaks, pines above the swamp that
littered my rented room with tipped shadow.

Give away the clothes that have kept me crouched: a young girl, I
already had boyfriends twice my age. By such slant alliances, trees
moved above the doorways, in rainy sequence hypogeal and fine. I
walked into myself and wrote down the same music she had sung

in another country, where we first lived, before men who chose me.
Note by note, the silt of rain and Byzantine keys.

About the Poet

PHOTO: Elisabeth Hogeman

C LAIRE MILLIKIN grew up in Georgia, North Carolina, and overseas. She received her BA in philosophy from Yale University, MFA in poetry from New York University, and PhD in English literature from the Graduate Center of the City University of New York. She currently teaches art history and sociology, as a lecturer at the University of Virginia.

Her poetry has appeared in numerous literary journals and magazines, including *Crab Orchard Review, Alabama Literary Review, North American Review, Iris: A Journal About Women, Willow Review, Ekphrasis, The Southern Poetry Review,* and *North Carolina Literary Review,* among others. Millikin has published the chapbook *The Gleaners* (Tiger's Eye Press, 2013), her first poetry collection, *Museum of Snow* (Grayson Books, 2013), and also *After Houses* (2Leaf Press, 2014), and *Motels Where We Lived* (Unicorn, 2014).

Millikin participates in numerous conferences, colloquia, presentations, and workshops around the country capturing a wide range of topics, including women's literature, femininity, gender and violence, gothic and ghosts, poverty, and race relations. Her fellowships, honors, and awards include Excellence in Diversity Fellow (Univ. of Virginia, 2011-2012); The Carolyn G. Heilbrun Dissertation Prize (2003); and The Helene Newstead Dissertation Year Fellowship (Graduate Center, CUNY, 2000-2002). Visit her website at http://www.claireraymond.org. ☀

OTHER BOOKS BY 2LEAF PRESS

2LEAF PRESS challenges the status quo by publishing alternative fiction, non-fiction, poetry and bilingual works by activists, academics, poets and authors dedicated to diversity and social justice with scholarship that is accessible to the general public. 2LEAF PRESS produces high quality and beautifully produced hardcover, paperback and ebook formats through our series: *2LP Explorations in Diversity, 2LP University Books, 2LP Classics, 2LP Translations, Nuyorican World Series,* and *2LP Current Affairs, Culture & Politics.* Below is a selection of 2LEAF PRESS' published titles.

2LP EXPLORATIONS IN DIVERSITY
Substance of Fire: Gender and Race in the College Classroom
by Claire Millikin
Foreword by R. Joseph Rodríguez, Afterword by Richard Delgado
Contributed material by Riley Blanks, Blake Calhoun, Rox Trujillo

Black Lives Have Always Mattered
A Collection of Essays, Poems, and Personal Narratives
Edited by Abiodun Oyewole

The Beiging of America:
Personal Narratives about Being Mixed Race in the 21st Century
Edited by Cathy J. Schlund-Vials, Sean Frederick Forbes, Tara Betts
with an Afterword by Heidi Durrow

What Does it Mean to be White in America?
Breaking the White Code of Silence, A Collection of Personal Narratives
Edited by Gabrielle David and Sean Frederick Forbes
Introduction by Debby Irving and Afterword by Tara Betts

2LP UNIVERSITY BOOKS
Designs of Blackness, Mappings in the Literature and
Culture of African Americans
A. Robert Lee
20TH ANNIVERSARY EXPANDED EDITION

2LP CLASSICS
Adventures in Black and White
Edited and with a critical introduction by Tara Betts
by Philippa Duke Schuyler

Monsters: Mary Shelley's Frankenstein and Mathilda
by Mary Shelley, edited by Claire Millikin Raymond

2LP TRANSLATIONS
Birds on the Kiswar Tree
by Odi Gonzales, Translated by Lynn Levin
Bilingual: English/Spanish

Incessant Beauty, A Bilingual Anthology
by Ana Rossetti, Edited and Translated by Carmela Ferradáns
Bilingual: English/Spanish

NUYORICAN WORLD SERIES
Our Nuyorican Thing, The Birth of a Self-Made Identity
by Samuel Carrion Diaz, with an Introduction by Urayoán Noel
Bilingual: English/Spanish

Hey Yo! Yo Soy!, 40 Years of Nuyorican Street Poetry,
The Collected Works of Jesús Papoleto Meléndez
Bilingual: English/Spanish

LITERARY NONFICTION
No Vacancy; Homeless Women in Paradise
by Michael Reid

The Beauty of Being, A Collection of Fables, Short Stories & Essays
by Abiodun Oyewole

WHEREABOUTS: Stepping Out of Place,
An Outside in Literary & Travel Magazine Anthology
Edited by Brandi Dawn Henderson

PLAYS
Rivers of Women, The Play
by Shirley Bradley LeFlore, with photographs by Michael J. Bracey

AUTOBIOGRAPHIES/MEMOIRS/BIOGRAPHIES
Trailblazers, Black Women Who Helped Make America Great
American Firsts/American Icons
by Gabrielle David

Mother of Orphans
The True and Curious Story of Irish Alice, A Colored Man's Widow
by Dedria Humphries Barker

Strength of Soul
by Naomi Raquel Enright

Dream of the Water Children:
Memory and Mourning in the Black Pacific
by Fredrick D. Kakinami Cloyd
Foreword by Velina Hasu Houston, Introduction by Gerald Horne
Edited by Karen Chau

The Fourth Moment: Journeys from the Known to the Unknown, A Memoir
by Carole J. Garrison, Introduction by Sarah Willis

POETRY
PAPOLíTICO, Poems of a Political Persuasion
by Jesús Papoleto Meléndez
with an Introduction by Joel Kovel and DeeDee Halleck

Critics of Mystery Marvel, Collected Poems
by Youssef Alaoui, with an Introduction by Laila Halaby

shrimp
by jason vasser-elong, with an Introduction by Michael Castro
The Revlon Slough, New and Selected Poems
by Ray DiZazzo, with an Introduction by Claire Millikin

Written Eye: Visuals/Verse
by A. Robert Lee

A Country Without Borders: Poems and Stories of Kashmir
by Lalita Pandit Hogan, with an Introduction by Frederick Luis Aldama

Branches of the Tree of Life
The Collected Poems of Abiodun Oyewole 1969-2013
by Abiodun Oyewole, edited by Gabrielle David
with an Introduction by Betty J. Dopson

2Leaf Press is an imprint owned and operated by the Intercultural Alliance of
Artists & Scholars, Inc. (IAAS), a NY-based nonprofit organization that publishes
and promotes multicultural literature.

NEW YORK
www.2leafpress.org